The
COMPLETE
Financial Directory

The Organizer Series

PO Box 443
Crosby, TX 77532

The Complete Financial Directory

The Organizer Series; Book 1

First Publication. Feburary 2010

ISBN 145056111X

EAN-139781450561112

Copyright © 2010

Table of Contents

Table of Contents

Notes

Introduction

It is a great idea to be prepared for the unexpected. This is why we purchase life insurance, auto insurance, and health insurance. Insurance was designed for being prepared. Everyone tries to be prepared for anything that can happen. The question is, what have you and your spouse not prepared for?

The truth is, for most couples, one person handles the finances and other 'administrative' duties of the household while the other usually tries to get away with knowing as little as possible about things such as insurance, bills, etc.

So, to find out if you need an organizational system in place ask yourself the following questions:

Does my spouse or loved one know where to locate our insurance policies?
Does my spouse or loved one know how our household bills are paid. Do they know how items are paid through your checking account? Are they aware of which bills are paid monthly and which are paid annually?
Do you feel as if your spouse or loved one may be lost without you?

Many couples answer no to most of these questions. It is unfortunate to feel this way. However, I am here to tell you that it is easy to change the answers to questions like these in your life. <u>Organization is key in truly being prepared.</u>

Picking up this book is the first step in getting yourself organized and getting your family on the right track – that is prepared for the unexpected. With piles of paperwork and no one prepared for a life altering event, it's time to organize your life! Once you have decided you are going to take the bull by the horns and organize your financial and life affairs for your loved one's benefit, it's time to find your means to peace.

Compiled of a series of easy to read forms, The Complete Financial Directory is, to my knowledge, the most extensive financial organizer on the market today. It's pages allow you to detail every aspect of your assets, liabilities and insurance.

This directory is essentially a shortened version of 'Your Complete Personal Directory'. It has been trimmed down to accommodate a less complicated method of organization for those consumers who don't necessarily need all of the extras. It's main focus is on financials such as assets, liabilities, and insurance. Of course, space has been provided for details on all subjects in the financial category and additional space has been provided throughout for notes and other details. This book is very similar to 'Your Complete Personal Directory' and is designed to be easy to read, easy to use, and customizable.

Introduction

By organizing your financials in this format, you are able to create an extensive picture of you finances to recall whenever you need it. It will not only be a valueable resource to your family if you should ever pass away, but it will also be useful in a multitude of other situations. Use it as your lifeline when paying bills, filing an insurance claim, or budgeting for tax payments.

Space has been provided for you to record the login information for all of your various accounts. Keep this handy when paying bills or managing your finances. You will find a plethora of information if you log into your profile at your service provider's website.

Use this directory as your own personal workbook. Remember, it is yours and the information stored within is for you. Don't be afraid to make it your own. Once you develop your own organizational habits, it will be easy for you to take the formats I have provided and fit them to your personal situation.

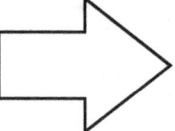 **You now have the power of organization on your side.**

Notes

Instructions

By purchasing this book, you have given yourself and your family one of the greatest gifts you could ever give them: the gift of information. Listed below are the final steps you must take to ensure that you are giving a complete gift. <u>Make sure you complete this process at least once every six months.</u>

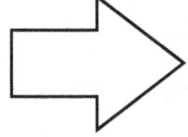 This book is divided into three major sections: Assets, Liabilities and Insurance. Take a moment to review the table of contents. Notate what sections apply to your situation. Not everything will apply. You may want to highlight the table of contents to indicate which sections you have completed.

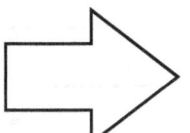 Gather all of your documents. You will want to locate bank statements, recent bills, tax returns, insurance policies, etc. Make sure you have all of your legal documents handy. This includes power of attorney document, birth certificates, wills, etc. Always use the most recent documents when updating this reference.

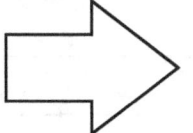 The first thing you need to do is fill out the following two pages. This is a 'Quick Reference Guide'. Made for you to be able to quickly locate important account numbers and phone numbers. List the names and phone numbers that you feel would be most important for you to be able to obtain quickly.

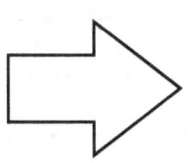 Complete all sections that apply to you. You may want to write in pencil so that you're information can be easily changed. This is especially true for website login information. Fill in every blank and make sure all of the information you input is as accurate as possible.

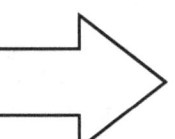 Choose a safe place to keep this book. A safe deposit box is recommended. However, if you plan to use this directory as a quick reference, it will need to be close at hand. If that is the case, I recommend a safe that is secured to the wall or floor of your home. Do not store this in a portable safe.

Quick Reference Guide

Business Type	Company Name	Account Number	Phone Number

Quick Reference Guide

Business Type	Company Name	Account Number	Phone Number

PART I

YOUR ASSETS

YOUR ASSETS

Notes

_____
_____
_____
_____
_____
_____
_____
_____
_____
_____
_____
_____
_____
_____
_____
_____
_____
_____
_____
_____

CHECKING

Ownership - Common ownership types include: Sole Owner, Joint with Right of Survivorship, Joint Tenants in Common, Trustee and Power of Attorney. Here you should indicate the Ownership type and who is listed on the account.

Routing Number - This is a number that is tied to your bank account. It is useful when setting up automatic debits and direct deposits on your account. You can obtain this number from the bottom of your check or by calling your financial institution.

Swift Code - Swift Codes are only used when recieving international wire transfers. You will most likely need to contact your financial institution to obtain the Swift Code for your account.

Naming a beneficiary - There is a beneficiary section for almost every account type throughout this book. It is very important that you name a beneficiary. If anything should happen to someone in your family, this will allow another party to step up and handle your finances.

Website Information - There is space for your to put your website login information for every account you hold. Use this with caution. Only store passwords in this directory if it is always secured away in a safe or safe deposit box.

Debit Card Number and PIN - Much like website login information, your debit card number and PIN are very sensitive pieces of information. If included, you should be sure to immediately store this book where it cannot get into the wrong hands.

Institution	Account Number
Ownership	Beneficiary
Address	http://
	Username
Phone Number	Password
Routing Number	Swift Code
Debit Card Number	PIN Number

Institution	Account Number
Ownership	Beneficiary
Address	http://
	Username
Phone Number	Password
Routing Number	Swift Code
Debit Card Number	PIN Number

Institution	Account Number
Ownership	Beneficiary
Address	http://
	Username
Phone Number	Password
Routing Number	Swift Code
Debit Card Number	PIN Number

SAVINGS ACCOUNTS

Ownership - Common ownership types include: Sole Owner, Joint with Right of Survivorship, Joint Tenants in Common, Trustee and Power of Attorney. Here you should indicate the Ownership type and who is listed on the account.

Naming a beneficiary - There is a beneficiary section for almost every account type throughout this book. It is very important that you name a beneficiary. If anything should happen to someone in your family, this will allow another party to step up and handle your finances.

Website Information - There is space for your to put your website login information for every account you hold. Use this with caution. Only store passwords in this directory if it is always secured away in a safe or safe deposit box.

ATM Card Number and PIN - Much like website login information, your debit card number and PIN are very sensitive pieces of information. If included, you should be sure to immediately store this book where it cannot get into the wrong hands.

Institution	Account Number
Ownership	Beneficiary
Address	http://
	Username
Phone Number	Password
ATM Card Number	PIN Number

Institution	Account Number
Ownership	Beneficiary
Address	http://
	Username
Phone Number	Password
ATM Card Number	PIN Number

Institution	Account Number
Ownership	Beneficiary
Address	http://
	Username
Phone Number	Password
ATM Card Number	PIN Number

Institution	Account Number
Ownership	Beneficiary
Address	http://
	Username
Phone Number	Password
ATM Card Number	PIN Number

CERTIFICATES OF DEPOSIT

Ownership - Common ownership types include: Sole Owner, Joint with Right of Survivorship, Joint Tenants in Common, Trustee and Power of Attorney. Here you should indicate the Ownership type and who is listed on the account.

Initial Deposit - Amount of money initially deposited into a single certificate.

Naming a beneficiary - There is a beneficiary section for almost every account type throughout this book. It is very important that you name a beneficiary. If anything should happen to someone in your family, this will allow another party to step up and handle your finances.

Website Information - There is space for your to put your website login information for every account you hold. Use this with caution. Only store passwords in this directory if it is always secured away in a safe or safe deposit box.

Interest Rate and Maturity Schedules - Use this table to update each individual CD. When renegotiating a CD, your account number should not change. A new interest rate and maturity date will be given and the information should be recorded here after each negotiation.

Institution		Account Number	
Ownership		Beneficiary	
Address		http://	
		Username	
Phone Number		Password	
Initial Deposit			

Details

Interest Rate	Maturity	Interest Rate	Maturity	Interest Rate	Maturity
	/ /		/ /		/ /
	/ /		/ /		/ /
	/ /		/ /		/ /
	/ /		/ /		/ /

Institution		Account Number	
Ownership		Beneficiary	
Address		http://	
		Username	
Phone Number		Password	
Initial Deposit			

Details

Interest Rate	Maturity	Interest Rate	Maturity	Interest Rate	Maturity
	/ /		/ /		/ /
	/ /		/ /		/ /
	/ /		/ /		/ /
	/ /		/ /		/ /

Institution	Account Number
Ownership	Beneficiary
Address	http://
	Username
Phone Number	Password
Initial Deposit	

Details

Interest Rate	Maturity	Interest Rate	Maturity	Interest Rate	Maturity
	/ /		/ /		/ /
	/ /		/ /		/ /
	/ /		/ /		/ /
	/ /		/ /		/ /

Institution	Account Number
Ownership	Beneficiary
Address	http://
	Username
Phone Number	Password
Initial Deposit	

Details

Interest Rate	Maturity	Interest Rate	Maturity	Interest Rate	Maturity
	/ /		/ /		/ /
	/ /		/ /		/ /
	/ /		/ /		/ /
	/ /		/ /		/ /

Institution	Account Number
Ownership	Beneficiary
Address	http://
	Username
Phone Number	Password
Initial Deposit	

Details

Interest Rate	Maturity	Interest Rate	Maturity	Interest Rate	Maturity
	/ /		/ /		/ /
	/ /		/ /		/ /
	/ /		/ /		/ /
	/ /		/ /		/ /

Institution	Account Number
Ownership	Beneficiary
Address	http://
	Username
Phone Number	Password
Initial Deposit	

Details

Interest Rate	Maturity	Interest Rate	Maturity	Interest Rate	Maturity
	/ /		/ /		/ /
	/ /		/ /		/ /
	/ /		/ /		/ /
	/ /		/ /		/ /

PRE-RETIREMENT

Ownership - Retirement plans generally only have one owner. Indicate who owns each retirement account in the 'Ownership' field.

HR Contact - Name of the Contact person at your Employer's Human Resources Department.

Naming a beneficiary - Most likely, your retirement plan requires you to designate a beneficiary. This is usually your spouse. If no beneficiary is designated the spouse usually becomes your automatic beneficiary.

Website Information - There is space for your to put your website login information for every account you hold. Use this with caution. Only store passwords in this directory if it is always secured away in a safe or safe deposit box.

Traditional or Roth - Most retirement plans through your employer are Traditional which means they deduct your contribution before taxes are taken from it. Roth plans take your contribution after taxes have already been paid on the money. Employers have just recently started offering the Roth account in addition to your Traditional Retirement Plan. Check with your HR department for details.

Plan Detail - Use this space to give additional details about your plan. Retirement plans can differ greatly. For example, does your plan offer in service withdrawls?

Institution		Account Number	
Ownership		Beneficiary	
Address		http://	
		Username	
Phone Number		Password	
Employer		HR Contact	
Account Type		☐ Roth	☐ Traditional
Plan Type	☐ 403(B) ☐ 401(K)	☐ Pension Plan	☐ Profit Sharing
	☐ Other _____		
Plan Detail			

Institution		Account Number	
Ownership		Beneficiary	
Address		http://	
		Username	
Phone Number		Password	
Employer		HR Contact	
Account Type		☐ Roth	☐ Traditional
Plan Type	☐ 403(B) ☐ 401(K)	☐ Pension Plan	☐ Profit Sharing
	☐ Other _____		
Plan Detail			

Institution		Account Number		
Ownership		Beneficiary		
Address		http://		
		Username		
Phone Number		Password		
Employer		HR Contact		
Account Type		☐ Roth		☐ Traditional
Plan Type	☐ 403(B) ☐ 401(K)	☐ Pension Plan		☐ Profit Sharing
	☐ Other _____			
Plan Detail				

Institution		Account Number		
Ownership		Beneficiary		
Address		http://		
		Username		
Phone Number		Password		
Employer		HR Contact		
Account Type		☐ Roth		☐ Traditional
Plan Type	☐ 403(B) ☐ 401(K)	☐ Pension Plan		☐ Profit Sharing
	☐ Other _____			
Plan Detail				

Institution	Account Number
Ownership	Beneficiary
Address	http://
	Username
Phone Number	Password
Employer	HR Contact

Account Type	☐ Roth	☐ Traditional
Plan Type ☐ 403(B) ☐ 401(K)	☐ Pension Plan	☐ Profit Sharing
☐ Other _____		

Plan Detail

Institution	Account Number
Ownership	Beneficiary
Address	http://
	Username
Phone Number	Password
Employer	HR Contact

Account Type	☐ Roth	☐ Traditional
Plan Type ☐ 403(B) ☐ 401(K)	☐ Pension Plan	☐ Profit Sharing
☐ Other _____		

Plan Detail

POST-RETIREMENT

Ownership - Retirement plans generally only have one owner. Indicate who owns each retirement account in the 'Ownership' field.

Naming a beneficiary - Most likely, your retirement plan requires you to designate a beneficiary. This is usually your spouse. If no beneficiary is designated the spouse usually becomes your automatic beneficiary.

Website Information - There is space for your to put your website login information for every account you hold. Use this with caution. Only store passwords in this directory if it is always secured away in a safe or safe deposit box.

Traditional or Roth - Most retirement plans through your employer are Traditional which means they deduct your contribution before taxes are taken from it. Roth plans take your contribution after taxes have already been paid on the money. Employers have just recently started offering the Roth account in addition to your Traditional Retirement Plan. Check with your HR department for details.

Plan Detail - Use this space to give additional details about your plan. Retirement plans can differ greatly. Space is provided to indicate if you have set up an IRA Money Market Account, Annuity, Brokerage, or other type of plan. Be specific with the details you give as these account differ extensively.

Institution	Account Number
Ownership	Beneficiary
Address	http://
	Username
Phone Number	Password
Account Type	☐ Roth ☐ Traditional
Plan Type	☐ MMA ☐ Annuity ☐ Brokerage
	☐ Other _____

Institution	Account Number
Ownership	Beneficiary
Address	http://
	Username
Phone Number	Password
Account Type	☐ Roth ☐ Traditional
Plan Type	☐ MMA ☐ Annuity ☐ Brokerage
	☐ Other _____

Institution	Account Number
Ownership	Beneficiary
Address	http://
	Username
Phone Number	Password
Account Type	☐ Roth ☐ Traditional
Plan Type	☐ MMA ☐ Annuity ☐ Brokerage
	☐ Other _____

Institution		Account Number		
Ownership		Beneficiary		
Address		http://		
		Username		
Phone Number		Password		
Account Type		☐ Roth	☐ Traditional	
Plan Type	☐ MMA	☐ Annuity	☐ Brokerage	
	☐ Other	_____		

Institution		Account Number		
Ownership		Beneficiary		
Address		http://		
		Username		
Phone Number		Password		
Account Type		☐ Roth	☐ Traditional	
Plan Type	☐ MMA	☐ Annuity	☐ Brokerage	
	☐ Other	_____		

Institution		Account Number		
Ownership		Beneficiary		
Address		http://		
		Username		
Phone Number		Password		
Account Type		☐ Roth	☐ Traditional	
Plan Type	☐ MMA	☐ Annuity	☐ Brokerage	
	☐ Other	_____		

Institution	Account Number
Ownership	Beneficiary
Address	http://
	Username
Phone Number	Password
Account Type	☐ Roth ☐ Traditional
Plan Type	☐ MMA ☐ Annuity ☐ Brokerage ☐ Other _____

Institution	Account Number
Ownership	Beneficiary
Address	http://
	Username
Phone Number	Password
Account Type	☐ Roth ☐ Traditional
Plan Type	☐ MMA ☐ Annuity ☐ Brokerage ☐ Other _____

Institution	Account Number
Ownership	Beneficiary
Address	http://
	Username
Phone Number	Password
Account Type	☐ Roth ☐ Traditional
Plan Type	☐ MMA ☐ Annuity ☐ Brokerage ☐ Other _____

TRADITIONAL INVESTMENTS

Ownership - Common ownership types include: Sole Owner, Joint with Right of Survivorship, Joint Tenants in Common, Trustee and Power of Attorney. Here you should indicate the Ownership type and who is listed on the account.

Naming a beneficiary - There is a beneficiary section for almost every account type throughout this book. It is very important that you name a beneficiary. If anything should happen to someone in your family, this will allow another party to step up and handle your finances.

Website Information - There is space for your to put your website login information for every account you hold. Use this with caution. Only store passwords in this directory if it is always secured away in a safe or safe deposit box.

Plan Detail - Use this space to give additional details about your plan. Investment plans can differ greatly from one another. Does your plan offer any tax advantages? Does it allow or restrict withdrawal?

Institution	Account Number
Ownership	Beneficiary
Address	http://
	Username
Phone Number	Password
Plan Type	☐ MMA ☐ Annuity ☐ Brokerage ☐ Other _____

Institution	Account Number
Ownership	Beneficiary
Address	http://
	Username
Phone Number	Password
Plan Type	☐ MMA ☐ Annuity ☐ Brokerage ☐ Other _____

Institution	Account Number
Ownership	Beneficiary
Address	http://
	Username
Phone Number	Password
Plan Type	☐ MMA ☐ Annuity ☐ Brokerage ☐ Other _____

Institution		Account Number		
Ownership		Beneficiary		
Address		http://		
		Username		
Phone Number		Password		
Plan Type	☐ MMA	☐ Annuity	☐ Brokerage	
	☐ Other			

Institution		Account Number		
Ownership		Beneficiary		
Address		http://		
		Username		
Phone Number		Password		
Plan Type	☐ MMA	☐ Annuity	☐ Brokerage	
	☐ Other			

Institution		Account Number		
Ownership		Beneficiary		
Address		http://		
		Username		
Phone Number		Password		
Plan Type	☐ MMA	☐ Annuity	☐ Brokerage	
	☐ Other			

Institution	Account Number
Ownership	Beneficiary
Address	http://
	Username
Phone Number	Password
Plan Type	☐ MMA ☐ Annuity ☐ Brokerage
	☐ Other _____

Institution	Account Number
Ownership	Beneficiary
Address	http://
	Username
Phone Number	Password
Plan Type	☐ MMA ☐ Annuity ☐ Brokerage
	☐ Other _____

Institution	Account Number
Ownership	Beneficiary
Address	http://
	Username
Phone Number	Password
Plan Type	☐ MMA ☐ Annuity ☐ Brokerage
	☐ Other _____

NON-TRADITIONAL INVESTMENTS

Ownership - Common ownership types include: Sole Owner, Joint with Right of Survivorship, Joint Tenants in Common, Trustee and Power of Attorney. Here you should indicate the Ownership type and who is listed on the account.

Naming a beneficiary - There is a beneficiary section for almost every account type throughout this book. It is very important that you name a beneficiary. If anything should happen to someone in your family, this will allow another party to step up and handle your finances.

Website Information - There is space for your to put your website login information for every account you hold. Use this with caution. Only store passwords in this directory if it is always secured away in a safe or safe deposit box.

Plan Detail - Use this space to give additional details about your plan. Investment plans can differ greatly from one another. Does your plan offer any tax advantages? Does it allow or restrict withdrawal?

Stock Certificates - Use this form to take an inventory of your paper stock certificates. Record the Company by name or symbol. Also record the number of shares owned, certificate number, and when it was purchased. All of this information should be listed on the front of the stock certificate.

Bonds - The most common types of paper bonds are govenment issued Series E, Series EE, Series H, and Series I. Use this form to record the bond type, face value, and maturity date.

Institution		Account Number	
Ownership		Beneficiary	
Address		http://	
		Username	
Phone Number		Password	
Plan Type	☐ 529	☐ Sweep Account	
	☐ Managed	☐ Other _____	
Other Details			

Institution		Account Number	
Ownership		Beneficiary	
Address		http://	
		Username	
Phone Number		Password	
Plan Type	☐ 529	☐ Sweep Account	
	☐ Managed	☐ Other _____	
Other Details			

Institution		Account Number	
Ownership		Beneficiary	
Address		http://	
		Username	
Phone Number		Password	
Plan Type	☐ 529	☐ Sweep Account	
	☐ Managed	☐ Other _____	

Institution	Account Number
Ownership	Beneficiary
Address	http://
	Username
Phone Number	Password
Plan Type	☐ 529 ☐ Sweep Account
	☐ Managed ☐ Other _____
Other Details	

Institution	Account Number
Ownership	Beneficiary
Address	http://
	Username
Phone Number	Password
Plan Type	☐ 529 ☐ Sweep Account
	☐ Managed ☐ Other _____
Other Details	

Institution	Account Number
Ownership	Beneficiary
Address	http://
	Username
Phone Number	Password
Plan Type	☐ 529 ☐ Sweep Account
	☐ Managed ☐ Other _____

Institution		Account Number	
Ownership		Beneficiary	
Address		http://	
		Username	
Phone Number		Password	
Plan Type	☐ 529	☐ Sweep Account	
	☐ Managed	☐ Other _____	
Other Details			

Institution		Account Number	
Ownership		Beneficiary	
Address		http://	
		Username	
Phone Number		Password	
Plan Type	☐ 529	☐ Sweep Account	
	☐ Managed	☐ Other _____	
Other Details			

Institution		Account Number	
Ownership		Beneficiary	
Address		http://	
		Username	
Phone Number		Password	
Plan Type	☐ 529	☐ Sweep Account	
	☐ Managed	☐ Other _____	

REAL ESTATE

Ownership - Here you should indicate who is on the deed of the property.

Primary Residence - Use this page to record details about your primary residence such as the year built, square footage, attached land, date it was purchased, and the number of bedrooms and baths. You may want to include other details. Do you have a homestead tax exemption? Does your home include a three car garage? Also included on this page is a form to record when items were replaced in your home such as your air conditioning unit, roof, or kitchen countertops.

Address (Primary)	**Year Built**
	Square Footage
Ownership	**Attached Land**
Date Purchased	**Number of Bedrooms / Baths**
Other Property Details	

Mortgaged?   ☐ **Yes**   ☐ **No**

Property Type   ☐ **Condo**   ☐ **Single Family Home**

                     ☐ **Other** _____

Address	**Year Built**
	Square Footage
Ownership	**Date Purchased**
Other Property Details	

Mortgaged?   ☐ **Yes**   ☐ **No**

Property Type   ☐ **Condo**   ☐ **Single Family Home**   ☐ **Land Only**

                     ☐ **Other** _____

Address	**Year Built**
	Square Footage
Ownership	**Date Purchased**
Other Property Details	

Mortgaged?   ☐ **Yes**   ☐ **No**

Property Type   ☐ **Condo**   ☐ **Single Family Home**   ☐ **Land Only**

                     ☐ **Other** _____

VEHICLES

Ownership - Here you should like who is on the auto loan or title of the vehicle.

Vehicle Specifics - There is room for information about six different vehicles. A quick reference for this information is your insurance policy. List the make, year, model, color, vin number, license plate number, and the date you puchased the vehicle.

Make	Model
Year	Color
Vin Number	License Plate Number
Ownership	Date Purchased
Location of Vehicle	

Lien? ☐ Yes   ☐ No

Vehicle Type ☐ Automobile ☐ ATV   ☐ Boat   ☐ Motorcycle
☐ Other _____

Make	Model
Year	Color
Vin Number	License Plate Number
Ownership	Date Purchased
Location of Vehicle	

Lien? ☐ Yes   ☐ No

Vehicle Type ☐ Automobile ☐ ATV   ☐ Boat   ☐ Motorcycle
☐ Other _____

Make	Model
Year	Color
Vin Number	License Plate Number
Ownership	Date Purchased
Location of Vehicle	

Lien? ☐ Yes   ☐ No

Vehicle Type ☐ Automobile ☐ ATV   ☐ Boat   ☐ Motorcycle
☐ Other _____

OTHER PROPERTY

Other Property - Space is provided here to list your valuable electronics and appliances. This information will become very valuable if there is a flood or fire. Also record warranty information for your higher ticket items. Usually, you should be able to obtain this information from the manufacturer.

Use the final page to record details about other valuable property such as jewlery and antiques.

Description of Property			Model Number	Serial Number	Date Purchased	Warranty? Yes No
Type	Make/Brand	Color				

Description of Property			Model Number	Serial Number	Date Purchased	Warranty?	
Type	Make/Brand	Color				Yes	No

Item	Description	Item Location

PART II

YOUR
INSURANCE

YOUR INSURANCE

Notes

LIFE INSURANCE

HR Contact - Name of the Contact Person at your Employer's Human Resources Department.

Insured - The insured is the person who's life is actually insured. Be sure to record the insured in this field and not the owner of the policy. The person who owns a policy is not always the insured.

Beneficiary - There is always a beneficiary listed on a life insurance policy. It is the individual who will recieve the death benefit when the insured dies.

Death Benefit - The monetary dollar amount a life insurance policy will pay when the insured dies.

Other Details - Be sure and include any details about your policy that makes it unique. The details of the following forms are suited to a Whole Life Insurance policy. If your policy is anything other than Whole Life or contains any special riders, be sure to include that in your description. This information will be valuable in helping your beneficary when making claims.

Website Information - There is space for your to put your website login information for every account you hold. Use this with caution. Only store passwords in this directory if it is always secured away in a safe or safe deposit box.

Insurance Company	Policy Number	
Insured	Beneficiary	
Address	http://	
	Username	
Phone Number	Password	
Death Benefit		
Annual Premium	Method of Payment	
Employer Sponsored Plan?	☐ Yes	☐ No
Employer	HR Contact	
Other Details		

Insurance Company	Policy Number	
Insured	Beneficiary	
Address	http://	
	Username	
Phone Number	Password	
Death Benefit		
Annual Premium	Method of Payment	
Employer Sponsored Plan?	☐ Yes	☐ No
Employer	HR Contact	
Other Details		

Insurance Company	**Policy Number**
Insured	**Beneficiary**
Address	**http://**
	Username
Phone Number	**Password**
Death Benefit	
Annual Premium	**Method of Payment**
Employer Sponsored Plan?	☐ Yes ☐ No
Employer	**HR Contact**
Other Details	

Insurance Company	**Policy Number**
Insured	**Beneficiary**
Address	**http://**
	Username
Phone Number	**Password**
Death Benefit	
Annual Premium	**Method of Payment**
Employer Sponsored Plan?	☐ Yes ☐ No
Employer	**HR Contact**
Other Details	

Insurance Company	Policy Number
Insured	Beneficiary
Address	http://
	Username
Phone Number	Password
Death Benefit	
Annual Premium	Method of Payment
Employer Sponsored Plan?	☐ Yes ☐ No
Employer	HR Contact
Other Details	

Insurance Company	Policy Number
Insured	Beneficiary
Address	http://
	Username
Phone Number	Password
Death Benefit	
Annual Premium	Method of Payment
Employer Sponsored Plan?	☐ Yes ☐ No
Employer	HR Contact
Other Details	

HOMEOWNER'S INSURANCE

Annual Premium - The amount paid annually to renew your homeowner's insurance policy.

Policy Limits - The limits to which your property is insured. There will be different limits listed for each type of damage. There will also be separate limits for contents and structural damage.

Website Information - There is space for your to put your website login information for every account you hold. Use this with caution. Only store passwords in this directory if it is always secured away in a safe or safe deposit box.

Insured Properties - Some insurance companies may allow you to carry more than one property on a single policy. So space has been provided for you to list each property that is insured within the policy.

Method of Payment - You will see this frequently throughout The Complete Financial Directory. There are several different ways a bill can be paid. Record your normal Method of Payment for each bill so that it will be easy to understand by a loved one. It is important that your bills continue to be paid on time even after you are gone. Everything will run more smoothly if your spouse knows how to continue paying your household bills.

Insurance Company	**Policy Number**
Address	**http://**
	Username
Phone Number	**Password**
Annual Premium	**Method of Payment**
Policy Limits	
Insured Properties	
Other Details	

Insurance Company	**Policy Number**
Address	**http://**
	Username
Phone Number	**Password**
Annual Premium	**Method of Payment**
Policy Limits	
Insured Properties	
Other Details	

Auto Insurance

Annual Premium - The amount paid annually to renew your homeowner's insurance policy.

Policy Limits - The limits to which your property is insured. There will be different limits listed for the various different causes of damage to a vehicle. Also, your auto insurance policy will have a separate limit for bodily injury.

Website Information - There is space for your to put your website login information for every account you hold. Use this with caution. Only store passwords in this directory if it is always secured away in a safe or safe deposit box.

Vehicles Insured - Some insurance companies may allow you to carry more than one vehicle on a single policy. So space has been provided for you to list each vehicle that is insured within the policy.

Method of Payment - You will see this frequently throughout The Complete Financial Directory. There are several different ways a bill can be paid. Record your normal Method of Payment for each bill so that it will be easy to understand by a loved one. It is important that your bills continue to be paid on time even after you are gone. Everything will run more smoothly if your spouse knows how to continue paying your household bills.

Insurance Company	**Policy Number**
Address	**http://**
	Username
Phone Number	**Password**
Annual Premium	**Method of Payment**
Describe Policy Limits	
Vehicles Insured	
Other Details	

Insurance Company	**Policy Number**
Address	**http://**
	Username
Phone Number	**Password**
Annual Premium	**Method of Payment**
Describe Policy Limits	
Vehicles Insured	
Other Details	

MEDICAL INSURANCE

Annual Premium - The amount paid annually to renew your homeowner's insurance policy.

HR Contact - Name of the contact personal at your employer's Human Resources Department.

Website Information - There is space for your to put your website login information for every account you hold. Use this with caution. Only store passwords in this directory if it is always secured away in a safe or safe deposit box.

Persons Insured - You may have a family plan which carries more than one person. List all persons covered by this plan.

Type of Insurance - Medical plans vary greatly. The forms provided are tailored to Health, Dental, and Vision plans. If your plan is different than what is listed, be sure and include specifics about it in the Other Details field.

Method of Payment - You will see this frequently throughout The Complete Financial Directory. There are several different ways a bill can be paid. Record your normal Method of Payment for each bill so that it will be easy to understand by a loved one. It is important that your bills continue to be paid on time even after you are gone. Everything will run more smoothly if your spouse knows how to continue paying your household bills.

Insurance Company	Policy Number
Address	http://
	Username
Phone Number	Password
Annual Premium	Method of Payment
Employer Sponsored Plan?	☐ Yes ☐ No
Employer	HR Contact
Type of Insurance: ☐ Health ☐ Vision ☐ Dental ☐ Other _____	
Persons Insured	
Other Details	

Insurance Company	Policy Number
Address	http://
	Username
Phone Number	Password
Annual Premium	Method of Payment
Employer Sponsored Plan?	☐ Yes ☐ No
Employer	HR Contact
Type of Insurance: ☐ Health ☐ Vision ☐ Dental ☐ Other _____	
Persons Insured	
Other Details	

MICELLANEOUS INSURANCE

Annual Premium - The amount paid annually to renew your homeowner's insurance policy.

HR Contact - Name of the contact personal at your employer's Human Resources Department

Website Information - There is space for your to put your website login information for every account you hold. Use this with caution. Only store passwords in this directory if it is always secured away in a safe or safe deposit box.

Persons Insured - You may have a family plan which carries more than one person. List all persons covered by this plan.

Type of Insurance - Insurance Plans vary greatly. If your plan is different than what is listed, be sure and include specifics about it in the Other Details field.

Method of Payment - You will see this frequently throughout The Complete Financial Directory. There are several different ways a bill can be paid. Record your normal Method of Payment for each bill so that it will be easy to understand by a loved one. It is important that your bills continue to be paid on time even after you are gone. Everything will run more smoothly if your spouse knows how to continue paying your household bills.

Insurance Company	Policy Number
Address	http://
	Username
Phone Number	Password
Annual Premium	Method of Payment
Type of Insurance:	☐ AD&D ☐ GAP ☐ Disability ☐ Other _____
Employer Sponsored Plan?	☐ Yes ☐ No
Employer	HR Contact
Describe coverage and Other Details	

Insurance Company	Policy Number
Address	http://
	Username
Phone Number	Password
Annual Premium	Method of Payment
Type of Insurance:	☐ AD&D ☐ GAP ☐ Disability ☐ Other _____
Employer Sponsored Plan?	☐ Yes ☐ No
Employer	HR Contact
Describe coverage and Other Details	

PART III

YOUR LIABILITIES

YOUR LIABILITIES

Notes

_____
_____
_____
_____
_____
_____
_____
_____
_____
_____
_____
_____
_____
_____
_____
_____
_____
_____
_____
_____

MORTGAGES

Lien holder - The financial institution that holds any lien against your property.

Collateral Address - The address of the property that secures the loan.

Website Information - There is space for your to put your website login information for every account you hold. Use this with caution. Only store passwords in this directory if it is always secured away in a safe or safe deposit box.

Method of Payment - You will see this frequently throughout The Complete Financial Directory. There are several different ways a bill can be paid. Record your normal Method of Payment for each bill so that it will be easy to understand by a loved one. It is important that your bills continue to be paid on time even after you are gone. Everything will run more smoothly if your spouse knows how to continue paying your household bills.

Due date and monthly payment amount - Not only is it important for your spouse to know how to pay your bills, but they should also know the due date and monthly payment amount for bills that are paid monthly. This information is also formatted for you to be able to use it as a quick reference for when you pay bills monthly.

Lien holder	Account Number
Phone Number	http://
Address	Username
	Password
Collateral Address	Due Date
	Term / Interest Rate
Monthly Payment Amount	Method of Payment

Lien Holder Position			☐ 1st	☐ 2nd	☐ 3rd
Loan Type	☐ FHA	☐ VA	☐ Heloc	☐ Heloan	☐ Conventional
	☐ Other				

Other Details

Lien holder	Account Number
Phone Number	http://
Address	Username
	Password
Collateral Address	Due Date
	Term / Interest Rate
Monthly Payment Amount	Method of Payment

Lien Holder Position			☐ 1st	☐ 2nd	☐ 3rd
Loan Type	☐ FHA	☐ VA	☐ Heloc	☐ Heloan	☐ Conventional
	☐ Other				

Other Details

AUTO LOANS

Lien holder - The financial institution that holds any lien against your property.

Website Information - There is space for your to put your website login information for every account you hold. Use this with caution. Only store passwords in this directory if it is always secured away in a safe or safe deposit box.

Method of Payment - You will see this frequently throughout The Complete Financial Directory. There are several different ways a bill can be paid. Record your normal Method of Payment for each bill so that it will be easy to understand by a loved one. It is important that your bills continue to be paid on time even after you are gone. Everything will run more smoothly if your spouse knows how to continue paying your household bills.

Due date and monthly payment amount - Not only is it important for your spouse to know how to pay your bills, but they should also know the due date and monthly payment amount for bills that are paid monthly. This information is also formatted for you to be able to use it as a quick reference for when you pay bills monthly.

Lien holder	Account Number
Address	http://
	Username
Phone Number	Password
Vehicle	Due Date
Term / Interest Rate	
Monthly Payment Amount	Method of Payment

Lien holder	Account Number
Address	http://
	Username
Phone Number	Password
Vehicle	Due Date
Term / Interest Rate	
Monthly Payment Amount	Method of Payment

Lien holder	Account Number
Address	http://
	Username
Phone Number	Password
Vehicle	Due Date
Term / Interest Rate	
Monthly Payment Amount	Method of Payment

OTHER LOANS

Lien holder - The financial institution that holds any lien against your property.

Website Information - There is space for your to put your website login information for every account you hold. Use this with caution. Only store passwords in this directory if it is always secured away in a safe or safe deposit box.

Method of Payment - You will see this frequently throughout The Complete Financial Directory. There are several different ways a bill can be paid. Record your normal Method of Payment for each bill so that it will be easy to understand by a loved one. It is important that your bills continue to be paid on time even after you are gone. Everything will run more smoothly if your spouse knows how to continue paying your household bills.

Due date and monthly payment amount - Not only is it important for your spouse to know how to pay your bills, but they should also know the due date and monthly payment amount for bills that are paid monthly.

Collateral - Some of your other loans may not have collateral. But if it does, space has been provided to describe the collateral.

Lien holder	Account Number
Phone Number	http://
Address	Username
	Password
Collateral	Due Date
	Term / Interest Rate
Monthly Payment Amount	Method of Payment
Loan Type ☐ Signature ☐ PLOC ☐ Personal ☐ Student ☐ ODLOC ☐ Other _____	
Other Details	

Lien holder	Account Number
Phone Number	http://
Address	Username
	Password
Collateral	Due Date
	Term / Interest Rate
Monthly Payment Amount	Method of Payment
Loan Type ☐ Signature ☐ PLOC ☐ Personal ☐ Student ☐ ODLOC ☐ Other _____	
Other Details	

CREDIT CARDS

Website Information - There is space for your to put your website login information for every account you hold. Use this with caution. Only store passwords in this directory if it is always secured away in a safe or safe deposit box.

Method of Payment - You will see this frequently throughout The Complete Financial Directory. There are several different ways a bill can be paid. Record your normal Method of Payment for each bill so that it will be easy to understand by a loved one. It is important that your bills continue to be paid on time even after you are gone. Everything will run more smoothly if your spouse knows how to continue paying your household bills.

Due date and monthly payment amount - Not only is it important for your spouse to know how to pay your bills, but they should also know the due date and monthly payment amount for bills that are paid monthly.

Credit Card Company	Account Number
Phone Number	http://
Address	Username
	Password
Interest Rate	Due Date
Monthly Payment Amount	Method of Payment

Credit Card Company	Account Number
Phone Number	http://
Address	Username
	Password
Interest Rate	Due Date
Monthly Payment Amount	Method of Payment

Credit Card Company	Account Number
Phone Number	http://
Address	Username
	Password
Interest Rate	Due Date
Monthly Payment Amount	Method of Payment

Credit Card Company	Account Number
Phone Number	http://
Address	Username
	Password
Interest Rate	Due Date
Monthly Payment Amount	Method of Payment

UTILITIES

Website Information - There is space for your to put your website login information for every account you hold. Use this with caution. Only store passwords in this directory if it is always secured away in a safe or safe deposit box.

Method of Payment - You will see this frequently throughout The Complete Financial Directory. There are several different ways a bill can be paid. Record your normal Method of Payment for each bill so that it will be easy to understand by a loved one. It is important that your bills continue to be paid on time even after you are gone. Everything will run more smoothly if your spouse knows how to continue paying your household bills.

Due date and monthly payment amount - Not only is it important for your spouse to know how to pay your bills, but they should also know the due date and monthly payment amount for bills that are paid monthly.

Payment Frequency - Utilitiy bills are sometimes paid less frequently than once a month. If that is the case for one of your utilities, indicate this on the following pages.

Company	Account Number
Phone Number	**http://**
Address	**Username**
	Password
Payment Frequency	**Due Date**
Monthly Payment Amount	**Method of Payment**

Utility Type ☐ Electricity ☐ Trash ☐ Water ☐ Home/Mobile Phone
☐ Internet ☐ HOA ☐ Gas ☐ Cable/Satellite TV
☐ Other _____

Other Details

Company	Account Number
Phone Number	**http://**
Address	**Username**
	Password
Payment Frequency	**Due Date**
Monthly Payment Amount	**Method of Payment**

Utility Type ☐ Electricity ☐ Trash ☐ Water ☐ Home/Mobile Phone
☐ Internet ☐ HOA ☐ Gas ☐ Cable/Satellite TV
☐ Other _____

Other Details

Company	Account Number
Phone Number	http://
Address	Username
	Password
Payment Frequency	Due Date
Monthly Payment Amount	Method of Payment

Utility Type	☐ Electricity	☐ Trash	☐ Water	☐ Home/Mobile Phone
	☐ Internet	☐ HOA	☐ Gas	☐ Cable/Satellite TV
	☐ Other			

Other Details

Company	Account Number
Phone Number	http://
Address	Username
	Password
Payment Frequency	Due Date
Monthly Payment Amount	Method of Payment

Utility Type	☐ Electricity	☐ Trash	☐ Water	☐ Home/Mobile Phone
	☐ Internet	☐ HOA	☐ Gas	☐ Cable/Satellite TV
	☐ Other			

Other Details

Company	Account Number
Phone Number	http://
Address	Username
	Password
Payment Frequency	Due Date
Monthly Payment Amount	Method of Payment

Utility Type ☐ Electricity ☐ Trash ☐ Water ☐ Home/Mobile Phone
☐ Internet ☐ HOA ☐ Gas ☐ Cable/Satellite TV
☐ Other _____

Other Details

Company	Account Number
Phone Number	http://
Address	Username
	Password
Payment Frequency	Due Date
Monthly Payment Amount	Method of Payment

Utility Type ☐ Electricity ☐ Trash ☐ Water ☐ Home/Mobile Phone
☐ Internet ☐ HOA ☐ Gas ☐ Cable/Satellite TV
☐ Other _____

Other Details

Company	Account Number
Phone Number	**http://**
Address	**Username**
	Password
Payment Frequency	**Due Date**
Monthly Payment Amount	**Method of Payment**

Utility Type ☐ Electricity ☐ Trash ☐ Water ☐ Home/Mobile Phone
☐ Internet ☐ HOA ☐ Gas ☐ Cable/Satellite TV
☐ Other _____

Other Details

Company	Account Number
Phone Number	**http://**
Address	**Username**
	Password
Payment Frequency	**Due Date**
Monthly Payment Amount	**Method of Payment**

Utility Type ☐ Electricity ☐ Trash ☐ Water ☐ Home/Mobile Phone
☐ Internet ☐ HOA ☐ Gas ☐ Cable/Satellite TV
☐ Other _____

Other Details

Company	Account Number
Phone Number	**http://**
Address	**Username**
	Password
Payment Frequency	**Due Date**
Monthly Payment Amount	**Method of Payment**

Utility Type	☐ Electricity	☐ Trash	☐ Water	☐ Home/Mobile Phone
	☐ Internet	☐ HOA	☐ Gas	☐ Cable/Satellite TV
	☐ Other			

Other Details

Company	Account Number
Phone Number	**http://**
Address	**Username**
	Password
Payment Frequency	**Due Date**
Monthly Payment Amount	**Method of Payment**

Utility Type	☐ Electricity	☐ Trash	☐ Water	☐ Home/Mobile Phone
	☐ Internet	☐ HOA	☐ Gas	☐ Cable/Satellite TV
	☐ Other			

Other Details

PROPERTY TAXES

Property Taxes - Keep detailed records of your property taxes. This is especially important if you own more than one property. Space has been provide to record important information about each property tax transaction. Also be sure to record which tax was paid. The most common types of property tax are state, county, and school.

Tax Year	Amount Paid	Payment Date	Property Address	Property Tax Paid
		/ /		☐ State ☐ County ☐ School ☐ Other
		/ /		☐ State ☐ County ☐ School ☐ Other
		/ /		☐ State ☐ County ☐ School ☐ Other
		/ /		☐ State ☐ County ☐ School ☐ Other
		/ /		☐ State ☐ County ☐ School ☐ Other
		/ /		☐ State ☐ County ☐ School ☐ Other
		/ /		☐ State ☐ County ☐ School ☐ Other
		/ /		☐ State ☐ County ☐ School ☐ Other
		/ /		☐ State ☐ County ☐ School ☐ Other
		/ /		☐ State ☐ County ☐ School ☐ Other
		/ /		☐ State ☐ County ☐ School ☐ Other
		/ /		☐ State ☐ County ☐ School ☐ Other
		/ /		☐ State ☐ County ☐ School ☐ Other
		/ /		☐ State ☐ County ☐ School ☐ Other
		/ /		☐ State ☐ County ☐ School ☐ Other

Tax Year	Amount Paid	Payment Date	Property Address	Property Tax Paid
		/ /		☐ State ☐ County ☐ School ☐ Other
		/ /		☐ State ☐ County ☐ School ☐ Other
		/ /		☐ State ☐ County ☐ School ☐ Other
		/ /		☐ State ☐ County ☐ School ☐ Other
		/ /		☐ State ☐ County ☐ School ☐ Other
		/ /		☐ State ☐ County ☐ School ☐ Other
		/ /		☐ State ☐ County ☐ School ☐ Other
		/ /		☐ State ☐ County ☐ School ☐ Other
		/ /		☐ State ☐ County ☐ School ☐ Other
		/ /		☐ State ☐ County ☐ School ☐ Other
		/ /		☐ State ☐ County ☐ School ☐ Other
		/ /		☐ State ☐ County ☐ School ☐ Other
		/ /		☐ State ☐ County ☐ School ☐ Other
		/ /		☐ State ☐ County ☐ School ☐ Other
		/ /		☐ State ☐ County ☐ School ☐ Other

Tax Year	Amount Paid	Payment Date	Property Address	Property Tax Paid		
		/ /		☐ State ☐ Other	☐ County	☐ School
		/ /		☐ State ☐ Other	☐ County	☐ School
		/ /		☐ State ☐ Other	☐ County	☐ School
		/ /		☐ State ☐ Other	☐ County	☐ School
		/ /		☐ State ☐ Other	☐ County	☐ School
		/ /		☐ State ☐ Other	☐ County	☐ School
		/ /		☐ State ☐ Other	☐ County	☐ School
		/ /		☐ State ☐ Other	☐ County	☐ School
		/ /		☐ State ☐ Other	☐ County	☐ School
		/ /		☐ State ☐ Other	☐ County	☐ School
		/ /		☐ State ☐ Other	☐ County	☐ School
		/ /		☐ State ☐ Other	☐ County	☐ School
		/ /		☐ State ☐ Other	☐ County	☐ School
		/ /		☐ State ☐ Other	☐ County	☐ School
		/ /		☐ State ☐ Other	☐ County	☐ School

INCOME TAXES

Income Taxas - Keep detailed records of your income taxes. Space has been provided to record important information about each tax transaction. The forms have been provided to record the basics of each year's tax return such as your total income, deductions, tax, etc.

Tax Year		
Dependents	**Exemptions**	
Filing Status	☐ Married Filing Jointly ☐ Married Filing Separately ☐ Head of Household ☐ Single ☐ Widow(er) ☐ Other _____	
Tax Type	☐ Federal	☐ State
Deductions	☐ Standard	☐ Itemized
Total Income	**Total Deductions**	
Total Tax	**Refund or Amount Owed**	
Other Details		

Tax Year		
Dependents	**Exemptions**	
Filing Status	☐ Married Filing Jointly ☐ Married Filing Separately ☐ Head of Household ☐ Single ☐ Widow(er) ☐ Other _____	
Tax Type	☐ Federal	☐ State
Deductions	☐ Standard	☐ Itemized
Total Income	**Total Deductions**	
Total Tax	**Refund or Amount Owed**	
Other Details		

Tax Year	
Dependents	**Exemptions**
Filing Status	☐ Married Filing Jointly ☐ Married Filing Separately ☐ Head of Household ☐ Single ☐ Widow(er) ☐ Other
Tax Type	☐ Federal ☐ State
Deductions	☐ Standard ☐ Itemized
Total Income	**Total Deductions**
Total Tax	**Refund or Amount Owed**
Other Details	

Tax Year	
Dependents	**Exemptions**
Filing Status	☐ Married Filing Jointly ☐ Married Filing Separately ☐ Head of Household ☐ Single ☐ Widow(er) ☐ Other
Tax Type	☐ Federal ☐ State
Deductions	☐ Standard ☐ Itemized
Total Income	**Total Deductions**
Total Tax	**Refund or Amount Owed**
Other Details	

Tax Year	
Dependents	**Exemptions**
Filing Status	☐ Married Filing Jointly ☐ Married Filing Separately ☐ Head of Household ☐ Single ☐ Widow(er) ☐ Other _____
Tax Type	☐ Federal ☐ State
Deductions	☐ Standard ☐ Itemized
Total Income	**Total Deductions**
Total Tax	**Refund or Amount Owed**
Other Details	

Tax Year	
Dependents	**Exemptions**
Filing Status	☐ Married Filing Jointly ☐ Married Filing Separately ☐ Head of Household ☐ Single ☐ Widow(er) ☐ Other _____
Tax Type	☐ Federal ☐ State
Deductions	☐ Standard ☐ Itemized
Total Income	**Total Deductions**
Total Tax	**Refund or Amount Owed**
Other Details	

Tax Year	
Dependents	**Exemptions**
Filing Status	☐ Married Filing Jointly ☐ Married Filing Separately ☐ Head of Household ☐ Single ☐ Widow(er) ☐ Other _____
Tax Type ☐ Federal ☐ State **Deductions** ☐ Standard ☐ Itemized	
Total Income	**Total Deductions**
Total Tax	**Refund or Amount Owed**
Other Details	

Tax Year	
Dependents	**Exemptions**
Filing Status	☐ Married Filing Jointly ☐ Married Filing Separately ☐ Head of Household ☐ Single ☐ Widow(er) ☐ Other _____
Tax Type ☐ Federal ☐ State **Deductions** ☐ Standard ☐ Itemized	
Total Income	**Total Deductions**
Total Tax	**Refund or Amount Owed**
Other Details	

Tax Year	
Dependents	**Exemptions**

Filing Status	☐ Married Filing Jointly	☐ Married Filing Separately
	☐ Head of Household	☐ Single ☐ Widow(er)
	☐ Other _____	

Tax Type	☐ Federal	☐ State
Deductions	☐ Standard	☐ Itemized

Total Income	**Total Deductions**
Total Tax	**Refund or Amount Owed**
Other Details	

Tax Year	
Dependents	**Exemptions**

Filing Status	☐ Married Filing Jointly	☐ Married Filing Separately
	☐ Head of Household	☐ Single ☐ Widow(er)
	☐ Other _____	

Tax Type	☐ Federal	☐ State
Deductions	☐ Standard	☐ Itemized

Total Income	**Total Deductions**
Total Tax	**Refund or Amount Owed**
Other Details	

UPDATES

Update this planner at least every six months. Update more frequently if required. After updates occurs, add the date to the table under the heading of the section that was updated. This way, by simply flipping to the back of The Complete Financial Directory, your and your family will immediately know how reliable and complete the information is inside.

Part I: Assets	Part II: Insurance	Part III: Liabilities
/ /	/ /	/ /
/ /	/ /	/ /
/ /	/ /	/ /
/ /	/ /	/ /
/ /	/ /	/ /
/ /	/ /	/ /
/ /	/ /	/ /
/ /	/ /	/ /
/ /	/ /	/ /
/ /	/ /	/ /
/ /	/ /	/ /
/ /	/ /	/ /
/ /	/ /	/ /
/ /	/ /	/ /
/ /	/ /	/ /
/ /	/ /	/ /
/ /	/ /	/ /
/ /	/ /	/ /
/ /	/ /	/ /
/ /	/ /	/ /
/ /	/ /	/ /
/ /	/ /	/ /
/ /	/ /	/ /
/ /	/ /	/ /

Part I: Assets	Part II: Insurance	Part III: Liabilities
/ /	/ /	/ /
/ /	/ /	/ /
/ /	/ /	/ /
/ /	/ /	/ /
/ /	/ /	/ /
/ /	/ /	/ /
/ /	/ /	/ /
/ /	/ /	/ /
/ /	/ /	/ /
/ /	/ /	/ /
/ /	/ /	/ /
/ /	/ /	/ /
/ /	/ /	/ /
/ /	/ /	/ /
/ /	/ /	/ /
/ /	/ /	/ /
/ /	/ /	/ /
/ /	/ /	/ /
/ /	/ /	/ /
/ /	/ /	/ /
/ /	/ /	/ /
/ /	/ /	/ /
/ /	/ /	/ /
/ /	/ /	/ /
/ /	/ /	/ /

Part I: Assets	Part II: Insurance	Part III: Liabilities
/ /	/ /	/ /
/ /	/ /	/ /
/ /	/ /	/ /
/ /	/ /	/ /
/ /	/ /	/ /
/ /	/ /	/ /
/ /	/ /	/ /
/ /	/ /	/ /
/ /	/ /	/ /
/ /	/ /	/ /
/ /	/ /	/ /
/ /	/ /	/ /
/ /	/ /	/ /
/ /	/ /	/ /
/ /	/ /	/ /
/ /	/ /	/ /
/ /	/ /	/ /
/ /	/ /	/ /
/ /	/ /	/ /
/ /	/ /	/ /
/ /	/ /	/ /
/ /	/ /	/ /
/ /	/ /	/ /
/ /	/ /	/ /

For more great products, visit our website at

http://www.simplypublished.com